INGA'S PRESENT

Written by Barbara Yeomans
Illustrated by Brian Lee

Collins Educational

An imprint of HarperCollinsPublishers

Chapter One

I remember that it was my birthday, my 11th birthday. I know it was a Thursday, and Dad wasn't there. Mum was trying to be jolly enough for two people, but it wasn't like other years, when they had both been there to give me a Happy Birthday hug and surround me while I opened all my presents.

Presents. It's because of the presents, or rather one particular present, that I remember that day even more distinctly. Mum had bought me a dress I'd wanted for ages, and Dad sent a note in my birthday card to say we could go out shopping on Saturday. I knew what I would choose. A radio. Then I could listen to the music I liked without Mum, or Dad, grumbling about it. Sometimes they did like a particular song, but mostly they seemed to think that nothing was quite as good as it was when they were young. The thing that really annoyed me was when a song came on the radio, and Mum would say, "Oh, the original version of that was much better. Hasn't anybody got any new ideas any more?"

Anyway, presents. Luckily, the postman came before I had to go to school. I wasn't really expecting anything in the post because most of my family lived quite near us, and came round specially to deliver presents. Even Dad must have put my card through the letter box himself, because there was no postmark on the envelope. I hated the thought that he had been so close, and hadn't come in. Perhaps he didn't really want to see me, as well as not wanting to see Mum. I kept thinking of all the times I'd been naughty and made him angry.

Brrrring! The doorbell made me jump while I was eating my cereal. Mum went to open the door and returned with a smallish package, wrapped in brown paper. It was addressed to me, in spidery handwriting I didn't recognise. The other thing I noticed was my full name written above the address, Miss Anna Perenna Ingram. Very grand, and odd, because not many people knew my real name. If anyone found out, they would only say, "What? How do you spell that?" and then I would wish I'd kept it to myself. Inga, my nickname, was quite bad enough. Why couldn't Mum and Dad have chosen a normal name for me? I rather fancied Zoe, though Harriet was nice too, except that people might call me Harry.

I undid the brown paper carefully. It was exciting to receive a real parcel in the post. Inside was a long, flattish, narrow box.

I lifted the lid, untwisted a lining of tissue paper, and found a fountain pen. It had a shiny blue casing which caught the light like the inside of mother-of-pearl sea shells, and the nib looked like silver. A proper fountain pen. But who had sent it to me? There was no little gift card, nothing to give me a clue. Mum was looking closely at the wandering writing on the brown paper.

"I think," she said slowly, "that this is your great-aunt Anna's writing. I'm sure she hasn't sent you anything for three or four years now. I wonder why she remembered this year. It's a beautiful pen. Fancy her doing that, and then not telling us who it's from."

Puzzling over the pen, we didn't notice time slipping on, until suddenly the radio intruded and reminded me that I must be leaving for school. It was a bright, windy March day and questions spun around my head as I went to the bus stop. Was the pen really from great-aunt Anna? What was she like? Why hadn't I met her? Did Dad know she'd sent me a present? And why couldn't

Dad be with us, especially on my birthday? Saturday felt a long way off. I missed his voice, and his big, comforting presence. The house didn't feel the same without him there.

Chapter Two

"Who is great-aunt Anna?" I asked Mum as soon as I got home from school. My thoughts had been whirling and wandering with the wind all day, and Mr Davis had told me off for not concentrating. Didn't teachers have special daydreams sometimes?

"I don't think you've ever met her," Mum replied as she filled the kettle. "She lives up in Cumbria, in the Lake District."

"Yes, but where does she belong in our

family?" I had the feeling that Mum was preoccupied. Her eyes were looking somewhere else.

"Anna is Dad's father's sister – your grandfather's elder sister. She must be about eighty by now. She's probably getting a bit forgetful; people often do as they get older." Mum went on making the tea. Our cat, Simpkin, twisted himself alarmingly round her legs as she moved. I always wondered how it was that we didn't step on him.

"Am I named after Aunt Anna?" It had only just struck me that we shared the same name. She surely would not have the same middle name. I had never heard of anybody called it before. It would be comforting if I was not the only one…

"Haven't I told you about that?" Mum asked as she poured tea into my favourite mug. "Yes, you are named after her, Anna Perenna. That's because you share the same birthday, the 15th of March. I remember when you were born, Dad said, "Beware the Ides of March!" Those are words from Shakespeare's play about Julius Caesar – you

know how much Dad likes Shakespeare –
and the Ides of March fell on the 15th of
March. I was a bit cross with him because
that's the day Caesar was assassinated and it
was such a happy day for us. So then he
suggested calling you Anna Perenna, after
his aunt, which was a much happier reason
to celebrate the 15th. It was a happy day for
the ancient Romans too, except for Caesar,
because it was the day they celebrated their
New Year, Anna Perenna. Their year began
on the 1st of March, and they celebrated
at the first full moon on the 15th. That is
where your aunt got her name in the
first place."

Talking about Dad often seemed to make
Mum grumpy, but I was curious about my
name and aunt Anna. I just wished adults
wouldn't choose names for such peculiar
reasons. I was glad when Mum went on,
"Yes, we wanted a name for you that was a
bit different, and it seemed just right for a
new member of the family… " she trailed
off. "You must thank great-aunt Anna for
the pen."

I wasn't very keen on thank-you letters. It was always so difficult to know what to write, especially when you didn't know the person.

"I'll do it at the weekend," I said, noticing too late that Mum had her no-arguments look on her face.

"You know you're going to see your father at the weekend," she reminded me – as if I'd forget. "Even if aunt Anna is old and forgetful, I'm sure she'd love to receive a letter from you, and you could show her that you're using the pen. You get that letter done tonight, then it won't be forgotten."

Mum was determined, so I decided not to protest, and anyway I was quite keen to try out the pen. After tea, I went to my room and got out the writing paper which Dad had given me when he went away.

"Even if Mum doesn't want you to phone me, you can still talk to me. Just write it down and send it," he had said. I felt a pang of guilt that the writing paper, with its border of cats, nose to tail, was still in its wrapping.

Chapter Three

I loved my bedroom. It was my own place, filled with my possessions. I had one of those blinds that falls in soft folds at the window which Dad had put up for my tenth birthday. The material had a border of cats on it, a bit like my writing paper, but these were chasing butterflies gathered in the central part of the blind. Sometimes, when I was going to sleep, I would imagine that I was one of the cats. I often chose a chunky black and ginger one, like Simpkin, our cat – and I would try to decide which butterfly to chase. I would never hurt the butterfly though, only imagine dabbing it softly with my paw, and the feel of its gossamer wings, flying away.

My bedroom was small, but there was just enough space at the foot my bed for a desk and my wheelchair. I felt important when I sat here and it was the place where I did most of my homework, and where I read my favourite books.

The rustle of writing paper as I opened the packet brought Simpkin into the room. He wound himself around the wheels of my chair, then bounced up onto the desk, where he began to wash his face. He licked one brindled paw and then wiped it over his ear and down his nose. I took my precious new pen out of its box and began to write our address at the top of the sheet of paper. Suddenly the busy paw shot out and tapped my hand holding the bright pen. Simpkin never could resist the crackle of crisp paper.

"Stop that. Keep your paws to yourself!"
His paw returned to its washing activities,
while I continued writing 'Dear A... '
Suddenly my hand was pushed violently, so
that I made a jerky line on the paper
instead of shaping the rest of 'Aunt'.

"Stop it!" This time I raised my voice. I
didn't want Simpkin's playfulness to ruin
my thank-you letter but he had retreated
softly to the back of the desk and sat,
hunched up like a trussed chicken. And his
ears had gone rather flat, as they did when
he met the next-door cat in his garden.
Something told me to carry on with the
letter but my hand felt twitchy, somehow
apart from me. As the pen met the paper,
my hand seemed to have a life of its own.
'*Anna*' it wrote, and the spiky writing was
not mine, but somehow familiar.

*It seems like the middle of the night, but
the clock tells me it is only half past nine.
There is a little bit of brightness left in the
sky, and the street lamp outside is giving
me just enough light to write. I dare not*

light a candle, it might wake Peter, and Mother says I must never ever light a candle when I am in bed. Where is she? The house is silent. I know that Father is on nights this week. He left the house while Peter and I were eating supper, a full three hours ago. Peter is sound asleep. Every now and then he twitches and reaches blindly for his toy bear. Bear's red and white ribbon is all twisted from the ravellings of Peter's night-time fingers.

Where is Mother? Something woke me; maybe the soft click of the front door closing. I've searched the house already. She is not here, not in the kitchen with her sewing, not in the bathroom putting cold cream on her face, certainly not in the bedroom. What shall I tell Peter when he wakes up? When will Father get home? Where is she?

As my hand wrote the last few words, it seemed to lose its independent power. It was my hand again, and my arm felt exhausted, stiff and cramped. I felt like I

did sometimes in the early morning, waking from a confused dream, not quite sure what was real. Bewildered, I folded the paper and put it away in my desk. Simpkin began to purr and shoved into me with his hard head, asking for attention. I left my bedroom with him at my wheels. Luckily, Mum was on the telephone, so I was able to slip into the sitting room and put the television on, unasked about my letter. Thursday was a good night, so I was looking absorbed when she returned from the telephone and I didn't hear any more about my thank-yous.

Chapter Four

On Friday nights I didn't usually go to my bedroom after tea as it was nice to think that homework could wait for once. This particular Friday was different though, with the thought of my desk seeming especially attractive. The telephone rang and Mum began a long, absorbed conversation with someone. She had never seemed to spend so much time on the phone when Dad was with us and I wasn't sure why she did now.

She still had me to talk to, after all, and I always did my best to keep her company.

I went to my room and there was the pen, lying on my desk where I had left it last night. I picked it up, found the cat-bordered paper, and started to write. Such an odd feeling came over me. The words I put down on the paper in that strange-familiar writing didn't seem to come from me. Someone was whispering in my head, suggesting, urgent. It was not really a frightening feeling, more like something I couldn't avoid, like brushing my teeth before going to bed. '*Anna*'. My name was on the paper again.

She has gone again — that same tiny sound woke me. Not a big slam like when Father goes out to work, but a private sound, not meant for anyone else to hear.

I must find her and bring her home to be with us. Peter is lying on Bear. I can see a shred of the ribbon and a paw sticking out under his arm. He seems peaceful. I'll tiptoe downstairs and look outside. Maybe

*she forgot to bring the washing in. That's
it, she is in the garden. She likes to water
the flowers in the evening. Says it is better
to water them when the hot sun has gone
from their leaves. She calls Peter and me
her best flowers when she tucks us up in
bed. But the back door is bolted. I cannot
see any familiar shape bending over the
borders. I'll look in the street. Perhaps she
has gone to see how Mrs Galloway is, with
her swollen rheumaticky joints. The front
door latch is stiff, the street deserted. There
is no-one outside. Peter cries out. I hope he
is dreaming, not awake and searching, too.
I must return upstairs.*

I dropped the pen suddenly, feeling
the overflowing sensation that comes just
before crying. Mum's voice penetrated
my confusion.

"Inga, have you done that letter yet? We
must post it in the morning."

"Yes, Mum," I said shakily. "I'll post it
when I go to meet Dad." Folding my
writing paper away again, I went into the

hall. Thinking about Dad calmed my mind,
and distracted me from brooding over the
writing. I wondered why Dad always had to
meet me at the end of our road. He had
spent years going in and out of this house.
Why couldn't he call for me, like my
friends did? Again, the thought that perhaps
he didn't really want to see me sneaked into
my mind. I vowed to be extra good this
weekend, not to make him impatient
or cross.

Chapter Five

I spent every other weekend with Dad.
He and Mum had split up just after my
tenth birthday, after he had put up that
blind in my bedroom. I suppose it had been
a relief in a way, because I had always hated
their arguments, the cruel words, and the
long, hostile, cold periods that followed.
The fights seemed to explode out of nothing,
like the volcanoes we'd seen on a video at
school. I'd try to delay bedtime, because it

was when I was in bed that the worst eruptions occurred. Of course my delaying tactics made them irritable too, but I didn't mind if it put off those angry voices. Surely they had loved each other once or why was I there? Why had they involved me in this? I wished my parents could be happy and laughing, like my friend Joanna's always were when I went round.

When I went to meet Dad, Mum would hurry me out of the house, as if she thought I was going to miss a bus.

"If he asks about me, just tell him I'm fine," she'd say and, sure enough, Dad would inevitably find some way of asking during the weekend, though he never said simply, "How's your mother?" Instead I would hear remarks like, "Mum's always got a good book on the go, hasn't she?" or "Mum never did like you to watch too much television." He said these things apologetically, as if he couldn't help mentioning her, and I was never sure what answer to give, so I usually pretended I hadn't heard.

That Saturday I was supposed to be posting my letter, but luckily Mum was more agitated than usual. She didn't seem to notice I wasn't carrying an envelope. Dad was there waiting at the end of the street and I got into his familiar red car. Weekends with him were like another life. He would ask me about school, and what I had done during the week, but when I answered him he could never remember the names of my teachers, or who my friends were. Half the time he seemed to be hardly listening to me. I felt like saying, "Hey, Dad. It's me, Inga. Did you really want to see me this weekend?" His new house was nearly an hour's drive away. It was small, disorganised, and didn't feel right. Sometimes I tried to tidy it up a bit for him, but he never seemed to notice. He would take me to the park, or sometimes to see a film. We often went to the library on Saturday afternoon. It was a big library and I nearly always found a good book which could occupy me for the weekend. There were so many things I wanted to tell Dad, but they wouldn't come out when I was with him. The words got lost inside me and it was easier to wrap myself up in a story.

I did mention the pen this weekend, though. After Dad bought me the radio, just the kind I wanted, he asked me what other presents I had received. I told him about the fountain pen.

"I'd like to see it. I could tell you for sure if it was aunt Anna's writing on the paper. She was my favourite aunt when I was little; she always sent a birthday present that was a little bit unusual. The other thing I remember is she couldn't stand cats. Said they knew too much."

I had to tell Dad that I had left the pen at Mum's house. I tried not to call it 'home' when I was with him. I had wanted to show him this strange present, but it didn't feel right to put it in my weekend bag. The pen seemed to belong on my desk and I had left it there, in the occasional care of Simpkin, who continued to flatten his ears every time he approached it.

Chapter Six

Monday was a bad day for being given homework. We had both English and Maths, and neither teacher ever forgot to give us some. We had been writing poems in English with Mr Davis, and homework was copying out the finished draft, and decorating it. For once I quite looked forward to the task. It would be another opportunity to use my new pen. I sat at my desk after tea, anticipating the satisfying feeling of completing a good piece of work. Poised above my English exercise book, however, my hand froze as I suddenly had the idea that I should copy out the poem on my cat-bordered paper. After all, the poem was about a cat, and we were supposed to decorate the final piece.

I drew the paper from my desk, and settled down, ready to write. But instead of my poem, I saw my own name appearing again, '*Anna*'.

> *This has been the worst day of my life. Now she has really gone, forever. Father has not gone to work tonight. He is sitting downstairs by the range doing nothing, just nothing. Why, why, why? They did not seem angry with one another - they never shouted. We finished our meal, and Mother stood up, cleared the dishes away into the scullery and then said, "That's it George. I have to go. My bags are packed and I am going to the station. Anna, Peter, my flowers, be good and help your father, and never forget that I love you."*

And he didn't try to stop her! He just put out his hand, but she shrank away as if his touch would burn her.

"If that's how it must be, Rose, so be it." That was all he said. Then she kissed Peter and me quickly and hurried out. He didn't try to stop her! Where has she gone now? Will we ever see her again? I helped Peter to wash his face and hands, and then I tucked him up in bed. He did not cry, just held Bear very tightly. Father said something about asking aunt Edie to come and stay for a while, but she won't know how we do things — when Peter is to go to bed, how to make Father's favourite herb dumplings, how to iron my best dress so the lace goes the right way.

Once again, I was forced to put down the pen as my eyes brimmed. Anna, Peter. I began to think about these two. I felt sure that Anna must be about my age. As for Peter, he must be younger. Perhaps the same sort of age as my friend Joanna's little brother, Mark. I had often heard Joanna teasing him about the big, grey rabbit which he took to bed with him each night... I had to find out what was going on, and it was Dad whom I needed to ask, not Mum. I needed to ask him that very moment, but of course he wasn't there. Why did parents have to behave so strangely? My head was ready to burst with questions, but I had to try to contain my impatience. When I finally left my room, I nearly bumped into Simpkin, draped like a rug just outside the sitting room door. Snapping at him, I thumped into a chair, knocking it over, and stared at the television.

"What has got into you?" enquired Mum.

"Nothing," I grumped. "My homework went wrong. I've had enough of it."

Chapter Seven

"Your aunt Anna, Dad," I said as soon as I met him on my next weekend visit, "has she got a brother called Peter?" Dad gave me a puzzled look.

"Well yes, of course. Your grandad's name is Peter. He's aunt Anna's younger brother. Why do you ask?"

I hadn't expected Dad to ask *me* questions, and avoided this one by asking another of my own.

"Is she, was she a happy person?" Dad was thoughtful.

"What a funny question, Inga. Why do you ask?" I was determined to solve my riddle, and all those days waiting to see Dad had made me even more impatient.

"Please, Dad, tell me. What happened to Anna's mother?" Dad's brow creased slightly, but his eyes were still smiling.

"Have I got a detective for a daughter?" He paused, but then went on. "I believe that grandad and aunt Anna's parents separated when Anna was about your age. Their mother met someone else and there was quite a scandal in the family because she left her husband and children for the other man."

"Why?" slipped out before I could stop it, but Dad carried on anyway as if he hadn't heard.

"My grandfather used to work nights, and I think Rose – your great-grandmother – must have felt very lonely. They said she was 'wayward', but I know that she was a very intelligent woman who loved to enjoy life. Maybe she felt trapped. I think what upset everyone most was she and George seemed so happily married. No-one suspected anything was wrong. Grandfather George was such an easy-going and amiable fellow."

Two questions still bothered me.

"How could great-grandmother have been lonely with her children there, and did Anna and Peter ever see their mother again?"

"It's probably hard for you to understand," Dad replied, "but sometimes adults need more than the company of their children, and I think she did try to come back to visit them, but life was different then. She wasn't made welcome in the town and after a time, grandfather remarried – my Nanna Lily – you know. Funny, another flower name. Lily couldn't bear to hear Rose's name mentioned, let alone allow her to come to the house. I don't really know what happened to Rose. I hope she was happy."

Sad though this was, I began to feel

happy that Dad was talking to me for once, about things that mattered. He was concentrating, sharing his thoughts. It eased the sadness of Anna's story.

"Anna never married. I believe she had a sweetheart, but he was killed in the war, and she went to live in the Lake District, to keep a small boarding house. She always loved the hills. She used to take me out for walks when I was a boy. She once said, "Can you feel the peace of these hills? That will never go away," and I felt smaller, younger, when I went to stay with her."

Dad stopped talking, and I was satisfied for the moment. He didn't ask me any more about my sudden curiosity, and I returned to Mum's house that Sunday evening wondering if I would find out any more about my great-aunt.

Chapter Eight

Going to bed that night, I realised that I hadn't thought of my cats chasing butterflies for a long time. Instead, I wondered about aunt Anna. I imagined her walking in the Lake District with Dad. I had never been there even though Dad and Mum had often promised to take me, but, when it was time to book holidays, Mum always chose.

"Somewhere warm," she would say. "You never know what the weather will do in the Lake District. Borrowdale is supposed to be the wettest place in England, and I don't fancy getting drenched every day."

My vision of the Lake District was, therefore, of a grey place, rather the shade of the slates on our roof: grey mountains, grey water. It suited my vision of aunt Anna as a sad, pensive young woman dressed in sensible walking clothes. It was difficult fitting Dad into the picture. To start with, I couldn't picture him as a little boy. He was fond of brightly-coloured clothes and it was difficult to see this lively small boy trotting along with aunt Anna in my slatey Lake District.

It was not until the middle of the week that the obvious course of action occurred to me and I was quite cross that it hadn't come to me before. I would give aunt Anna the chance to tell me more, herself. I could hardly wait to get home from school.

At last tea time was over, and Mum was safely on the telephone leaving Simpkin and me to escape to the privacy of my bedroom. Simpkin began his evening wash while I took up my pen, unfolded the paper and waited. This time there was no tell-tale flattening of Simpkin's ears, no tingling feeling in my hand or arm. Bother! It looked like I would have to do some History homework after all – we were learning about the Second World War and our task was to imagine being a child evacuated from home. I was enjoying the topic and it was fun to try to be someone else, to try out another point of view. I took my History exercise book from my school bag and started to write the title, 'Diary of… ' But now came that uncontrollable liveliness in my hand and I found I had written '*Diary of Anna P*'. Simpkin had stopped washing and was watching me intently.

Today I saw David off on the train. He looked so smart in his uniform, laughing and joking with the other men. His face changed when he turned to me though, "I'll be home on leave soon. The time will fly by. You will be true to me, Anna, won't you? This war will be over soon, and then we'll be married and I won't have to go away again."

The words spilled out fast, as if he had to say all these important things while there was still time. I smiled and hugged him. Of course I'll be true. I have known him so long. Our two fathers worked together. I remember my first sight of him was when he came round to our house one early evening, just before my Father left for work.

"My father's not well tonight. He won't be going to work and Mother says, could you tell the boss?" I remember his words because I always felt a sharp twinge of jealousy when someone mentioned their Father and Mother together. Well, he has gone, and now I'll count the days until we are together again. I am so tired today.

My hand became immobile. Poor Anna! She had lost those two vitally important people. Why was life so unfair? Some people seemed to have no difficulties, no sadness, while others received more than

their fair share. I thought again of my friend Joanna. Always full of funny stories, ready for any adventure at school, her happy Mum and Dad safely at home in their elegant house. Yes, even the house felt lucky. It was always beautiful, with a bowl of fresh flowers on the table. It was like one of those houses you see in magazines in the dentist. Charmed lives, I thought.

Chapter Nine

Another good thing about my birthday was that it always meant that the Easter holidays were not far away. Once it was Easter I could feel that the cold days were almost over for another year. Evenings were lighter and Joanna and I could meet and go out after school. Racing along, propelled only by myself, with a little help from the wind, I liked to compare myself to the April clouds skimming the earth, seeing everything.

Holidays, of course, meant no regular homework, and so I had no reason to pick up my fine pen. Nor did I feel any compulsion to use it. It lay safely resting in its little box, snug in a groove on a raised, moulded base. It reminded me of the figures carved on top of tombs in old churches.

Then, one day – it was Ash Wednesday – a letter came in the post. Mum hesitated before she opened the envelope because it was addressed to her and Dad together. Everyone knew that my mum and dad had split up, I thought, so I was curious about the contents of the envelope. Who could be so undiplomatic? Mum's expression was hard to decipher as she read the short typed letter.

"This concerns you, Inga," she said finally. "It seems that your great-aunt Anna died last week, peacefully in her sleep. The letter is from a solicitor in Kendal, who is looking after her Will. I can hardly believe it, but she has left you her home in the Lake District." Mum paused.

"Does it say anything else?" I demanded, full of attention.

"It says that you are to have the house, so that you may feel the peace of the hills, that will never go away. How strange." Mum was puzzled, but I knew why those words were there and felt a flash of happiness. Aunt Anna had sent me a final, comforting message. Mum had a little more to read.

"The solicitor writes that aunt Anna had requested a simple cremation, and that she wished for her ashes to be scattered over the fell behind her house. Her wishes are being carried out today."

I felt peaceful that great-aunt Anna could rest and that my pen had told its tale. Then Mum carried on, "Your father and I are responsible for the house until you are old enough, Inga. I'll have to talk to him so that we can try to reach some sort of agreement about what to do. I'll phone him now."

To my surprise, Mum went straight to the telephone and dialled Dad's work number. She'd never before phoned him in

front of me. I was even more startled when, after a short conversation, she actually suggested that he should come to the house to discuss the problem properly. He was picking me up the next evening anyway – I was to spend a long Easter weekend with him – so they apparently agreed that that was the obvious opportunity for a talk. Mum's cheeks looked a bit pink when she put the phone down, as if she had been caught doing something she shouldn't. I was so excited I offered to make her a cup of coffee, something I normally did only grudgingly or when she looked especially tired.

Next day I was in my room packing before breakfast. Simpkin was 'helping' as he always did, trying to sit on every article of clothing I tried to fold. My stomach reminded me finally that I should go and eat, and I went to the kitchen to find Mum on the telephone again. She was saying, "I quite understand. I'm so sorry. Yes, it will be best," and my heart started to beat very fast. I immediately assumed that there was some hitch about aunt Anna's Will, "my" house. I was wrong.

"That was Joanna's Mum," said mine when she had put the phone down. "Jo and her brother are going to come and stay with us for a few days when you get back from Dad's."

"Great!" I said. It was always fun to have Jo to stay. We would see how long we could stay awake at night, whispering to each other under the bedclothes. Then, "Why on earth is Mark coming?" I asked as the thought struck me. "What is there for him to do here? He'll just trail after us with his rabbit."

"I'm afraid Joanna's Mum and Dad are having a few problems," Mum explained. "Jo and Mark are coming here to give them all a break so they can try to sort things out."

Jo's Mum and Dad! I knew the meaning of those phrases 'having a few problems' and 'sort things out' only too well. I had heard them so often when Dad moved out of our house. I knew how much hurting they disguised.

"You'll have to try to be extra nice to Mark and look after him a bit," said Mum.

I suddenly felt quite kindly towards Jo's formerly annoying little brother. Yes, I would try to help him, as Anna helped Peter. I felt almost guilty for the feeling of intense relief that their family was not perfect either.

The day passed in anticipation of Dad's arrival. As the clock approached the appointed time, I grew more and more nervous. I could hardly bear the thought of the two of them talking together again, in this house, but apart. I pretended that I had forgotten to pack some vital treasures and hid in my bedroom after Dad arrived. I tried not to hear their voices, as I had done before when they argued. The old, feared increase in volume did not happen though, and it was not long before I heard Mum shout up the stairs.

"Inga, have you packed your thick socks and jumpers?" I emerged to find them both waiting in the hall, smiling.

"Come on girl," Dad said. "If we get
a move on, we'll be in the Lake District
in time to see those hills get up in
the morning."